AURORA

Remember ... Life is for learning what you intuitively feel is right for you at this present moment in time ... Tomorrow is another day!

'Love', 'Light' and 'Peace'

JAN

AURORA

Magnetic Crystal Sound Healing

JAN LINCH

(Edited by Jenny Fairmam)

HAVEN PUBLISHERS
MAIDSTONE · KENT

Published by Haven Publishers
P.O. Box No. 901, Sutton Valence, Maidstone,
Kent ME17 3PN, England

First published in 2000

Text and illustrations copyright © Jan Linch

Cover photograph: Jan Curtis
Illustrations: Geoffrey Curd

The right of Jan Linch to be identified as the author of this work has been asserted by her in accordance with the Copyright, Designs and Patents Act 1988

The author of this book has no connection with the medical profession and, therefore, does not provide medical advice or advise that any person should cease taking any medical treatments from their doctor. The author and publisher accept no legal responsibilities for any actions that the reader may choose to take relating to any matters contained in this book

Some of the contents within this book have been taken from the book *Starchild* (ISBN. 0 9535417 0 3) by the same author

All rights reserved

No part of this publication may be reproduced by any means or in any form whatsoever without written permission from the publishers, except for brief quotations involved in literary reviews or articles

ISBN 0 9535417 2 X

Designed by Merriton Sharp, London
Printed by Thanet Press Limited, Margate, Kent

Contents

List of illustrations	vi
Preface	vii
1 Aurora Magnetic Crystal Sound Healing	1
2 The Auric Colours and the Chakras	6
3 Magnet Therapy	23
4 Crystals and their Healing Potential	27
5 Healing with Sound	34
6 The Therapeutic Use of Aurora Bottles	48
Recommended Reading	53

Illustrations

Opposite page

1	The Traditional Chakra System with Sound	8
2	The Geometrical Chakra System with Sound	9
3	The Traditional Complementary Colour Wheel with Sound	24
4	The Geometrical Complementary Colour Wheel with Sound	25

Preface

Aurora was brought into being by two alternative therapists who work as spiritual teachers, lecturers, healers and authors. Although they were well acquainted with each other, it took a rather unusual trip to Sedona in Arizona to recognise that both of them had been channelling the same spiritual inspirations for many months.

It is believed by both therapists that the extraordinary spiritual powers of Sedona encouraged them to understand, on a profound level, how their combined knowledge and personal energies could create a new healing system that could help many people to heal themselves.

Jan Linch has been working as a colour therapist and healer for ten years and more recently has been teaching about colour, sound, crystals and magnets. Jan has always been fascinated by colour since childhood and her recently published book *Starchild* explains many interesting details about her work with colour.

Pamela Couchman has been a colour therapist, lecturer and healer for five years and has lectured on colour, crystals and energies in many parts of Kent including a local college of further education. Pamela is also a Reiki Master.

1

Aurora Magnetic Crystal Sound Healing

In Roman mythology Aurora was the name given to the goddess of the dawn (otherwise known as Eos). Aurora had a lover called Tithonus, who later became her husband and wishing to be bound to him for eternity, Aurora begged Jupiter (the leader of the gods) for Tithonus to have eternal life. But she had forgotten to ask Jupiter at the same time for perpetual youth and as the years passed her young and handsome husband became old and wrinkled. Aurora, in shame, hid Tithonus away in a chamber until she finally begged Jupiter to do something. After much begging Jupiter relented and Tithonus was changed into a cicada (grasshopper).

The word 'aurora' has been taken from the name aurora borealis/australis. The luminous electrical radiation from the northern or southern magnetic poles are called aurora borealis and aurora australis respectively. They are often called aurora, aurorae or northern or southern lights because they can be seen from either hemisphere as beautiful rays of light that create many different colours. These coloured lights occur when particles of energy from the sun become trapped in the Earth's magnetic field and when this happens the trapped energy begins to vibrate at many different frequencies. It is this form of vibration that creates the colours. Vibration of light/colour is also linked to sound and it is known that the aurora lights create different sounds – from gentle ethereal sounds to subtle crackling sounds. Because Aurora (the goddess of the dawn) is linked to colour and light she, too, is linked to the vibration of sound and the sounds that come with the dawn of each new day.

With the dawning of a new age it is, therefore, appropriate that Aurora Magnetic Crystal Sound Healing is a combination of four alternative therapies – Colour, Magnets, Crystals and Sound. Because the word 'aurora' is linked to coloured lights I have used Aurora throughout this book to represent the alternative therapy related to colour. The individual alternative therapies can be dated back to the ancient Egyptians and the Chinese who used coloured essential oils for therapeutic massage and healing. Crystals and sound were used widely and it is thought that Cleopatra wore magnets and crystals to keep her healthy and youthful. A more detailed explanation on each individual therapy is to be found later on in the book under their separate chapters.

Aurora has beautifully hand-decorated coloured bottles. Each bottle has relevant coloured crystals attached around the neck. The bottles sit in a base that holds six north-facing magnets (see Chapter Three – Magnet Therapy). The base is designed to hold a tuning fork that has a sound frequency relevant to the colour. The bottles can be filled with a base oil or aromatherapy oils for massage, or water for drinking purposes. The magnets magnify the effect of the healing powers within the crystals and also the vibration of each relevant sound and colour. Water and oils are very good conductors for carrying this healing energy, created from colour, magnets, crystals and sound. Once the water has been drunk or the oils massaged into the physical body, the coloured, magnetic, crystal, sound energy within the water or the oils can start to work instantly through the physical body, thus putting back its natural magnetic balance. Each bottle is quite unique in its colours, crystals, sounds and magnetics because each bottle has different healing powers that vibrate at different healing frequencies. It is these healing frequencies that resonate with the same frequencies as those of the chakras. The chakras are energy centres that feed and protect the physical body. They vibrate at different frequencies in order to maintain and balance good health within the major organs. Each bottle is also unique in other ways such as, each one carries its own name and message and the message is quite often linked to the person who is magnetically drawn to it

Aurora bottles can heal on a physical, emotional, mental and spiritual level of consciousness. Different bottles can help to heal different illnesses and most of the time you will find that you will be magnetically drawn to a bottle or bottles that you need to heal yourself and thus put back your own balance. Balance can be achieved by working through the negative aspects in your life to find the positive aspects. The healing bottles can help you to eliminate the negative and encourage the positive aspects in your life on all levels of consciousness.

Aurora can offer you versatility. You can either select a ready-made-up bottle of your choice or choose your own colour, crystals and sound. The bottles come with or without magnets, crystals or sound. The bottles can be made to suit each individual's needs because it is recognised that, like the bottles, each individual is unique and each individual's needs will be different on all levels of consciousness.

The beautiful coloured bottles can also be used for colour readings and simple analysis. Colour consultations can be given on a physical, emotional, mental and spiritual level of consciousness which can include subconscious mysteries of the past, present and future energies, giving each individual an idea as to his/her purpose in life. The coloured bottles that you are drawn to act like magnets, attracting you to the colours that you are and the colours that you need. You will quite often find that the colours you are magnetically drawn to are also linked to the colours within your aura, your true colours. The colours within your aura can often answer many questions as to why you are here and what your purpose is in life.

In a reading, you will be asked to select a minimum of four coloured combination bottles from a wide selection.

The colours that are chosen will be a true mirror of the self, a recognition of the deep need within the being which colours your life. The colours that are selected reflect like a mirror image the true colours of the aura, the soul, and the higher consciousness. The higher consciousness acts like a spiral, which continues its journey in the form of a spiral from the beginning of time to eternity. The colours contain a personal record. As fingerprints are the identity kit of the person, so the auric colours are the identification of the soul essence. All the previous experiences from the beginning of time can leave their mark upon the true colours of the aura. Therefore, the aura becomes a map and a record of the true personality and imparts the complete soul sense and recognition of one for another. It is through aura recognition that the old soul recognises those with whom he or she has travelled. Thus twin souls meet, soul mate meets soul mate and the foreknowledge from the depth of the being ... knows.

Anything that impedes the progress of the self leaves its scar and thus creates a sick aura. It is this that is nearly always the root cause of sickness on a physical, emotional, mental and spiritual level of consciousness.

Once Aurora is put into use either by drinking the energised water from the bottle or by massaging the physical body with aromatherapy oils from the bottles, the energy can begin to work immediately. The bottles are very powerful because they contain four alternative therapies in one – colour, magnets, crystals and sound.

You will be magnetically drawn to the colours you are and the colours you need.

The first bottle that you are drawn to is linked to your chosen mission.

The second bottle that you are drawn to is linked to your past.

The third bottle that you are drawn to is linked to your present.

The fourth bottle that you are drawn to is linked to your future.

All of the bottles show aspects linked to karma and lessons. All of the bottles show how many of the masters, angels and unseen entities will be helping, guiding and protecting you throughout your mission and on your life's journey. All of the bottles show past life links and possible repetitive patterns from them. All of the bottles show your positive aspects and gifts that are often hidden. The bottles also show if you have been hanging on to any past difficulties and can often indicate what those difficulties might be. An Aurora therapist would also be able to advise on a bottle that would help to release these difficulties.

Please note, an Aurora therapist can only act as a guide because this alternative therapy is meant to be non-intrusive. You choose the colours that you are and also the colours that you need on all levels of consciousness.

2

The Auric Colours and the Chakras

The aura is a protective energy field that surrounds the physical body like an egg. It has many layers to it which go out approximately fifty-five feet or more on the Earth alone. The aura acts like a computer. It collects data and holds within it all the information of each lifetime of the soul, and it can be read just like a book. All the information within the aura is also within the subconscious mind, that ninety percent of the brain that you don't use. The aura can help you to recognise other souls with whom you have walked before. It can help you to recognise your gifts that will be helping you with your mission in this lifetime, along with your difficulties, lessons and karma. It shows the repetitive patterns through each incarnation.

The aura carries within it colours, some of which have never been seen in this dimension. That is, they are vibrating at such a high frequency of light, that the brain is not always capable of seeing them. The colours in your aura are just light that is vibrating at different frequencies. It is these colours that have a remarkable effect on your personality, for these colours make you the person that you are. Your true colours. The fingerprints of your soul.

Many incarnations can leave the aura exhausted and thus create many scars within it. These scars show within the aura in the form of etheric gaps which can often be seen as dark patches. These dark patches are also known as negative or dark ectoplasm.

You have colours in your aura that can vibrate at a positive or a negative frequency. When you are feeling good then the coloured energies within your aura vibrate in a positive way, thus keeping you healthy. When you are feeling low or down then the coloured energies within your aura vibrate in a negative way, thus making you feel ill or out of balance. You have the choice whether you want to work with the positive side to those colours or the negative side. The idea is to work through the negative to achieve the positive.

Within the auric egg there is what is called the chakra system. The chakras are energy centres which feed and protect the physical body both front and back. Each chakra is there to protect the major organs of the body. The chakras vibrate at different colour frequencies and it is these colour frequencies that are fed through the chakra system and into the relevant organs. When healthy the chakras are perfectly cone-shaped. When your chakras are healthy and in balance then you, too, are healthy and in balance.

Because each chakra vibrates at a different colour frequency it can attract both positive and negative aspects of those colours, whether spiritual, emotional, or physical. If a chakra is placed out of balance by having to work through a negative aspect then this can cause a chain reaction, which can affect the spiritual, emotional and physical level of being.

As you work through the negative aspects, the chakras can become out of balance until you can begin to bring in the positive aspects, which should then put them back into balance again. There will be times when you will have to work through the negative to achieve the positive. This is all part of your spiritual growth.

In the past you may have come across seven of the major chakras that are linked to the colours of the rainbow – Red, Orange, Yellow, Green, Blue, Indigo and Violet. This chakra system is the old traditional system that many therapists still successfully work with. However, more recently there have been many more helpful books that you can purchase on additional colours and new chakras. Some writers of these books believe that the new chakras are not new at all and that the chakras have always been there, latent, waiting to be awakened. These new or latent chakras form part of a new geometrical chakra system (geometrical because they can be measured). These new or latent chakras can be found simply by measuring the distance between the outer edge of the eyes (approximately 10cm). The geometrical chakra system shows twelve chakras that are located on the front and back of the body. A thirteenth chakra lies just outside the body above the head. As the new or latent chakras begin to awaken within you they will bring in and attract different colours. As with all colours, you will begin to attract the positive and the negative frequencies that come with them.

If you look at Diagram One (opposite page 8) you will see how colour and sound can work with the old traditional chakra system. If you look at Diagram Two (opposite page 9) you will see how additional colours and sounds can work with the new geometrical chakra system.

The colours that relate to the chakras are listed in Table 1. The list shows both the old (traditional) and the new (awakening latent) ones and how the chakras are connected to the major organs or glands of the physical body. Some chakras are connected to more than one organ or gland. The thirteenth chakra (in the new awakening chakra system) lies just above the crown and is the beginning of the many diverse astral chakras. The thirteenth chakra is the beginning of a whole new octave.

Colours can help to heal you spiritually, emotionally and physically, which helps to maintain a colourful balance within the chakras as well as the aura. There are numerous ways that you can put back your balance by using colour. The colour within your home might not have been chosen by coincidence. If you chose the colours within your home décor those colours might be just what you need. If you do not have a choice with regards your surrounding décor you could try visualising colour through meditation. The colours that you wear or even the

Violet 7 = B

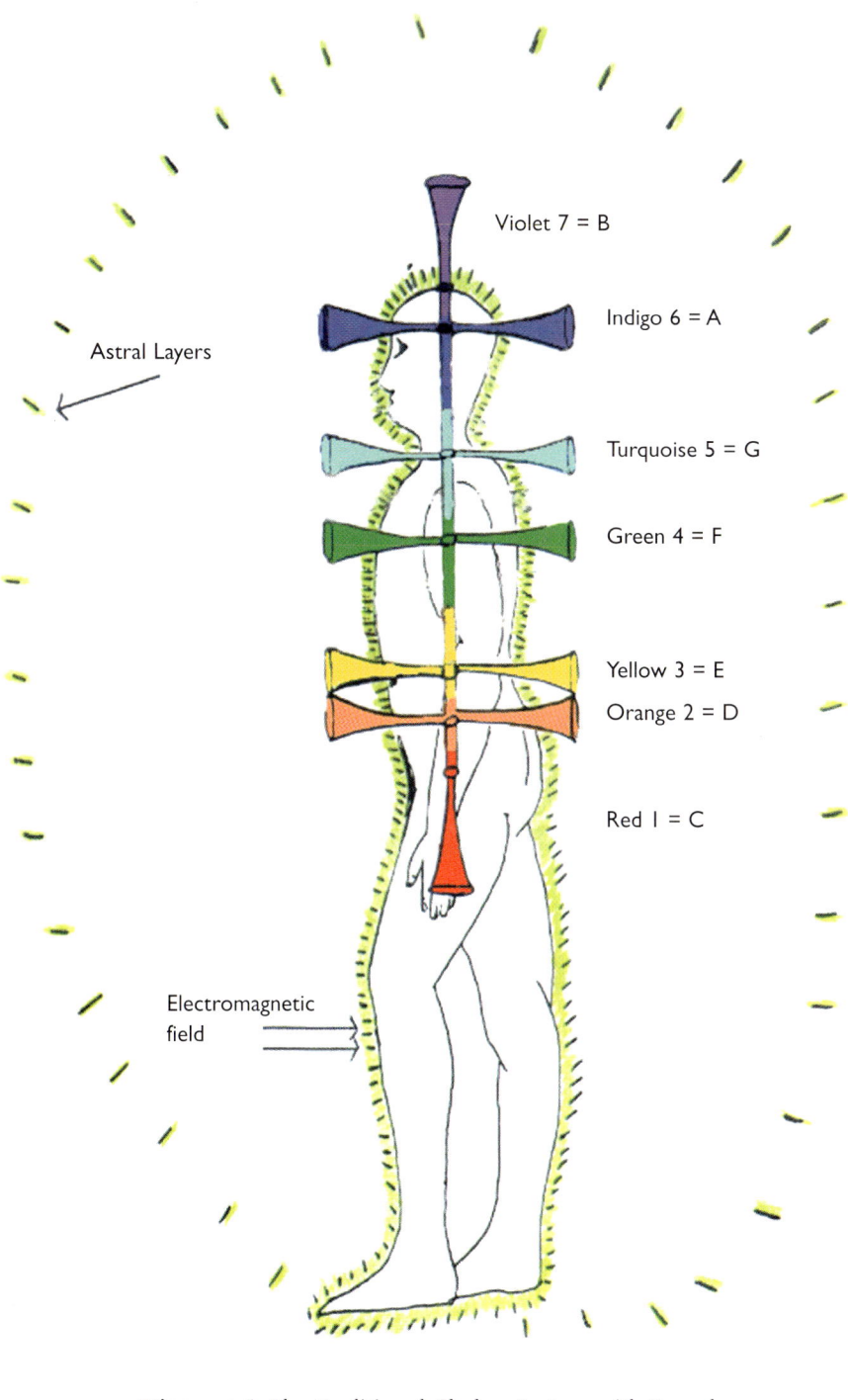

Indigo 6 = A

Astral Layers

Turquoise 5 = G

Green 4 = F

Yellow 3 = E
Orange 2 = D

Red 1 = C

Electromagnetic field

Diagram 1 The Traditional Chakra System with Sound.

Magenta 13 = C

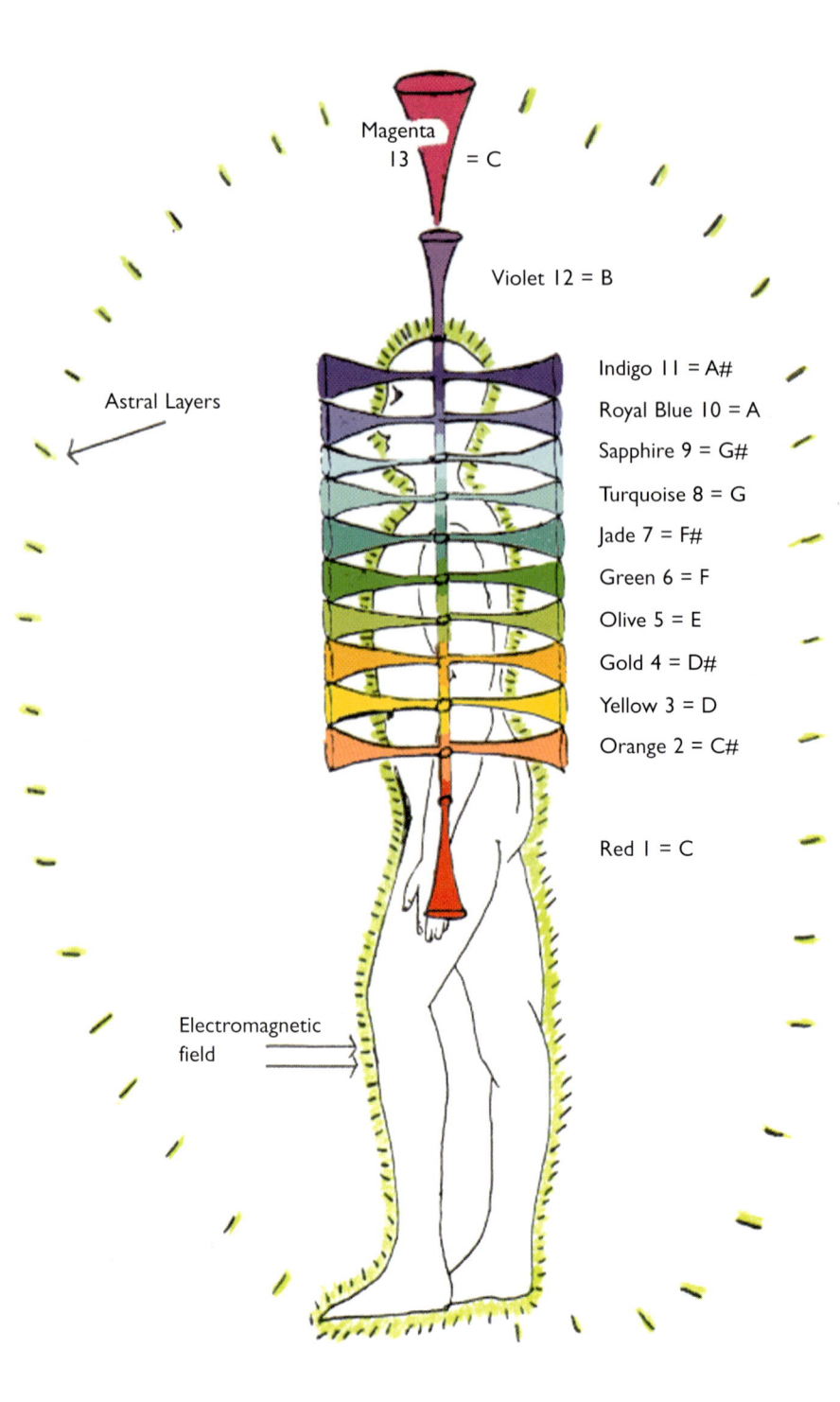

Violet 12 = B

Indigo 11 = A#
Royal Blue 10 = A
Sapphire 9 = G#
Turquoise 8 = G
Jade 7 = F#
Green 6 = F
Olive 5 = E
Gold 4 = D#
Yellow 3 = D
Orange 2 = C#

Red 1 = C

Astral Layers

Electromagnetic field

Diagram 2 The Geometrical Chakra System with Sound.

The Auric Colours and the Chakras

Table 1 Colours relating to the chakras

Red
Gonads
The gonads of the male sex glands are the testes.
The first chakra, known as the Base, is situated between the pubic bone and the coccyx.
First in the traditional chakra system.
First in the new awakening chakra system.

Orange
Gonads/Adrenals
The gonads of the female sex glands are the ovaries.
Two adrenal glands are situated at the upper end of each kidney. They produce important hormones like adrenalin and corticosteroids.
The second chakra, known as the Sacral, is situated in the lower abdomen area.
Second in the traditional chakra system.
Second in the new awakening chakra system.

Yellow
Pancreas
A gland in the abdomen behind the stomach which aids the digestive system. It also acts as an endocrine gland, secreting insulin into the blood as a hormone.
The third chakra, known as the Solar Plexus, is situated within the navel. It is also known as the Umbilical Cord of Spirituality.
Third in the traditional chakra system.
Third in the new awakening chakra system.

Gold
Pancreas
The fourth chakra, known as the Golden Star or Diamond within the centre of your being, is situated in the diaphragm area.
Does not always feature in the old traditional chakra system.
Fourth in the new awakening chakra system.

Olive
Heart and Lungs
The fifth chakra, known as the Lower Heart Chakra, is situated at the xiphisternum or free end-bone of the rib cage.
Does not feature in the old traditional chakra system.
Fifth in the new awakening chakra system.

Table 1 *continued*

Green   Heart and Lungs
              The sixth chakra, known as the Heart Chakra, is situated in the centre of the sternum.
              Fourth in the traditional chakra system.
              Sixth in the new awakening chakra system.

Jade   Thymus
              The thymus is a small gland behind the upper part of the breast bone which produces lymphocytes and is believed to play an important part in the development of the body's immune system. It is situated just below the area where the two clavicle bones meet at the upper end of the sternum.
              The seventh chakra, known as the Upper Heart Chakra, is situated at the upper part of the breastbone.
              Does not feature in the traditional chakra system.
              Seventh in the new awakening chakra system.

Turquoise   Thyroid
              The thyroid gland is an endocrine gland at the base of the neck. It secretes hormones necessary for the development of the growth of the body. It controls the metabolism and levels of calcium in the blood to ensure efficient development of the bones.
              The eighth chakra, known as the Throat Chakra, is situated at the throat.
              Fifth in the traditional chakra system.
              Eighth in the new awakening chakra system.

Sapphire   Tongue and Senses
              The tongue is a muscular organ in the mouth which links the many senses through communication on many levels of consciousness.
              The ninth chakra, known for its spiritual protection, is situated at the tip of the chin.
              Does not feature in the traditional chakra system.
              Ninth in the new awakening chakra system.

The Auric Colours and the Chakras

Table 1 *continued*

Royal Blue	Cerebellum (large part of the brain)
	Situated in the rear part of the skull, the cerebellum's main function is the coordination of balance through muscle control.
	The tenth chakra, known as the Well of Dreams, is situated at the tip of the nose and is also linked to the ears.
	Does not feature in the old traditional chakra system.
	Tenth in the new awakening chakra system.
Indigo	Pineal
	The pineal gland is shaped like a pine cone, and is situated behind the third ventricle of the brain. Its function is linked to the body clock, distinguishing night and day. It could also be linked to a sixth sense. It may be possible that the pineal gland is responsible for helping us to see the three dimensional magic eye pictures.
	The eleventh chakra, known as the Third Eye, is situated in the centre of the forehead between the eyes and is also linked to the eyes.
	Sixth in the traditional chakra system.
	Eleventh in the new awakening chakra system.
Violet	Pituitary
	The pituitary gland is a gland at the base of the brain, which produces hormones to aid the functioning of the other endocrine organs in the body.
	The nerve impulses within the brain can send messages to other parts of the body at over two hundred miles per hour!
	The twelfth chakra, known as the Crown, is situated at the top of the head.
	Seventh in the traditional chakra system.
	Twelfth in the new awakening chakra system.
Magenta	The Astral – Just above the Crown.
	Linking Heaven and Earth.
	Does not always feature in traditional chakra systems.
	Thirteenth in the new awakening chakra system.

colours of the food you eat can help you to put back your own colour balance. Colour therapists often heal by visualising colour or using coloured torches. Some therapists advise on colours to wear whilst others will suggest coloured massage oils.

Aurora Magnetic Crystal Sound Healing bottles have been created to help people to put back their own healing balance within their physical body, aura and chakras, naturally. You are not only drawn to the colours that make you the person that you are, but you are also drawn to the colours that you need to heal yourself. Through self-selection the choice of a beneficial healing bottle is your own, thus it becomes a non-intrusive therapy. There may be more than one colour decorating the bottles of your choice. This is your choice and, therefore, shows your needs as well as your personality.

Listed in Table 2 are some of the positive and negative traits that are linked to the many colours that Aurora apply in their readings and healing. The list indicates why you were (or are) perhaps drawn to specific colours and also how the star signs can be connected to the colours. The list also shows how different colours can be used to heal on all levels of consciousness.

As you go through the positive and negative aspects of each colour you will begin to recognise some of the lessons or karma that you might have already learned or gone through. You might recognise that you are now bringing in and working with the positive traits linked to the colours below.

Ideally, you need the vibration of every positive colour in your aura in order to keep the chakras in balance because this will help to keep you physically balanced and well. If you do not like a specific colour, it could be a subconscious way of avoiding the negative traits that go with it. For instance, if you dislike the colour red it may be that you dislike anger, frustration and the ego. If you don't bring red into your aura you may lack energy, passion, optimism and enthusiasm for life. You may even suffer with lower back problems, or poor blood circulation.

Table 2 Positive and negative traits linked to colours

Red	Red is linked to Aries, Gemini, Virgo, Scorpio and Sagittarius.

Positive Aspects: Survival, being full of energy, optimism, enthusiasm and passion.

Negative Aspects: Anger, frustration, power and control, ego, sarcasm, materialism and greed.

Physical vulnerabilities are lower back and poor blood circulation.

Red combination bottles should only be used below the waist and avoided if you have heart problems or high blood pressure. Use an orange combination instead.

The frequency of the colour red is effective for stimulating underactive conditions. Red gives you energy and is good for impotence and it stimulates the desire, passion, optimism and enthusiasm for life. It is a very energising colour that is good for the blood and blood circulation. It is also good for the lower back.

Orange   Orange is linked to Taurus, Leo, Sagittarius and Aquarius.

Positive Aspects: Warmth, bliss, joy, humour, confidence, courage, freedom, aspiration, wisdom and sunshine.

Negative Aspects: Shock, trauma, sadness, loneliness, dependency, confusion, fear and lack of confidence.

Physical vulnerabilities are hormones, colon, spleen, gall bladder and bladder.

The frequency of the colour orange is effective for shock, fear and trauma. It is also effective on the spleen, hormones and lower abdomen. Orange gives you sunshine, happiness and joy and it brings warmth and confidence into your life. Because orange has the hidden colours of red and yellow within, it can convey the same healing qualities as those colours.

Table 2 *continued*

Yellow Yellow is linked to Gemini, Leo, Virgo, Scorpio and Capricorn.

Positive Aspects: Knowledge, intellect, praise, happiness, optimism and a love of animals.

Negative Aspects: Nervous fear, anxiety, stress and exaggeration.

Physical vulnerabilities are the digestive tract, pancreas, kidneys, liver and urinary tract.

The frequency of the colour yellow is effective for nervous fear. The skin is often affected through nervous fear and yellow has a very good healing frequency for this. It is also effective on the liver, kidneys, stomach, gall bladder and digestive tract, all of which are affected by nervous stress and anxiety. In fact, yellow is very healing for the whole nervous system. Yellow can stimulate knowledge, intellect, optimism and praise.

Gold Gold is linked to Aries, Gemini, Leo and Virgo.

Positive Aspects: Wisdom, philosophy, deep bliss and warmth.

Negative Aspects: Deep fears, anxiety and confusion.

The physical vulnerabilities are the digestive tract, pancreas, kidneys, liver and urinary tract.

The frequency of the colour gold is linked to wisdom and philosophy. Because gold has the hidden colours of red, orange and yellow within, it can convey the same healing qualities of those colours. Gold can help you to use your energy with wisdom.

The Auric Colours and the Chakras

Table 2 *continued*

Olive Olive is linked to Taurus, Gemini, Cancer, Virgo, Libra, Sagittarius, Capricorn, Aquarius and Pisces.

Positive Aspects: Emotional independence and finding joy through Earth changes.

Negative Aspects: Emotional confusion and fear of Earth changes.

The physical vulnerabilities are the heart and lungs.

The frequency of the colour olive is good for emotional confusion, emotional shock, trauma, stress, indecisiveness and misdirection. Olive is good for balancing the heart and lungs. Olive can help you to put back emotional wisdom and balance in your life. Because olive has the hidden colours of green and gold within, it can also convey the same healing qualities of those colours.

Green Green is linked to Taurus, Gemini, Cancer, Virgo, Libra, Sagittarius, Capricorn, Aquarius and Pisces.

Positive Aspects: Balance, harmony, heart-felt feelings, being in touch with nature, sincerity, trust, justice and generosity.

Negative Aspects: Envy, suspicion, guilt, dishonesty, argumentativeness, being judgemental and fears of change.

The physical vulnerabilities are the heart and lungs.

The frequency of the colour green is good for putting you back into balance and harmony. Green helps you to overcome lack of trust, guilt, envy and judgement. Green is effective for the heart, lungs, thymus and emotional stress. Green is also good for balancing the blood and blood pressure. Green will also put you in your own space, thus it is very effective for those suffering from phobias, particularly claustrophobia. Because green has the hidden colours of yellow and blue within, it can convey the same healing qualities of those colours.

Table 2 *continued*

Jade	Jade is linked to star signs with green, turquoise and gold within.

Positive Aspects: Artistic communication from the heart and teaching from the heart.

Negative Aspects: Fear of communicating the truth from the heart.

The physical vulnerabilities are the thymus, heart and lungs.

Jade can help you to learn as well as teach the truth through wisdom and philosophy of the heart. Jade is effective for the thymus and the immune system. Because jade has the hidden colours of green, turquoise and gold within, it can convey the same healing qualities as those colours. |
| *Turquoise* | Turquoise is linked to Taurus, Gemini, Cancer, Leo, Libra, Sagittarius, Aquarius and Pisces.

Positive Aspects: Peace, confidence, beauty, art, music and writing.

Negative Aspects: Lack of peace, lethargy, communication difficulties.

The physical vulnerabilities are the throat and thyroid gland.

The frequency of the colour turquoise is effective for the throat and vocal chords. Turquoise is linked to the breath and can, therefore, help those suffering from asthma, chest infections and bronchitis. Turquoise can stimulate truth that comes from the heart, helping you to communicate what you truly feel from the heart. Because turquoise has the hidden colours of green and yellow within, it can convey the same healing qualities as those colours. |

The Auric Colours and the Chakras

Table 2 *continued*

Sapphire	Sapphire is linked to Taurus, Gemini, Cancer, Leo, Libra, Sagittarius, Aquarius and Pisces.

Positive Aspects: Spiritual protection and spiritual communication.

Negative Aspects: Fear of spiritual contact and lack of ambition.

The physical vulnerabilities are the throat and senses.

Sapphire is linked to spiritual protection and, like the turquoise, it is linked to the breath. Sapphire calms the breath – you are born on an in-breath and die on an out-breath. Sapphire is effective for calming the breath especially when the heart has been exerted perhaps through spiritual fears. Sapphire can help you to put spiritual confidence into your life without fear. Because the colour sapphire has the hidden colours of green and yellow within, it can convey the same healing qualities of those colours.

Royal Blue	Royal Blue is linked to Aries, Taurus, Cancer, Virgo, Scorpio, Capricorn, Aquarius and Pisces.

Positive Aspects: Deep peace and a good listener.

Negative Aspects: Poor listener, being absentminded and often stubborn.

The physical vulnerabilities are the ears, eyes, nose, throat, teeth and brain.

The frequency of the colour royal blue can aid with memory loss especially when you want to remember your dreams. Royal blue has a healing effect on the ears, eyes, nose, throat and teeth, as well as the brain.

Table 2 *continued*

Indigo	Indigo is linked to Aries, Taurus, Cancer, Virgo, Scorpio, Capricorn, Aquarius and Pisces.
	Positive Aspects: Clairvoyance, clairaudience and good intuition.
	Negative Aspects: Superstition, negative thinking and often being disorderly.
	The physical vulnerabilities are the ears, eyes, nose, throat, teeth and brain.
	Indigo is effective for the mind, poor memory, balance (including vertigo) and clumsiness. Indigo can help to ease problems associated to the ears, eyes, nose, throat and teeth, as well as the brain. Because indigo has the hidden colour of gold within, it can convey the same healing quality of that colour.
Violet	Violet is linked to Aries, Libra, Scorpio, Sagittarius, Capricorn, Aquarius and Pisces.
	Positive Aspects: Spiritual healing, devotion and dedication.
	Negative Aspects: The worrier, snobbery, a low self-esteem, domination, arrogance and abuse of spiritual power.
	Physical vulnerability is the head.
	Violet is linked to the head and any head conditions. Violet is very healing and can create a calm relaxed energy within a stressful mind. Violet is effective for any head conditions such as headaches, migraines, insomnia and stress through worry. Because violet has the hidden colours of red and blue within, it can convey the same healing qualities of those colours.

Table 2 *continued*

Magenta	Magenta is an astral colour linked to the Christ consciousness and the awakening of the Christ consciousness on Earth.

Positive Aspects: Divine healing through divine love.

Negative Aspects: The dreamer, often one who lives in a world of his/her own.

Physical vulnerability is lack of energy because of being un-earthed.

The frequency of the colour magenta is effective for putting back the love that may have been lost through a divine healing. When you cannot find love on the physical level then magenta links you in with the divine energy to bring down love from Heaven to Earth. This colour is Heaven on Earth and the need for it. Because magenta has the hidden colours of red (which is the Earth colour) and violet (which is the Heavenly colour) within, it can convey the same healing qualities of those colours. |
| *Pink* | Pink is linked to Aries, Cancer, Libra, Capricorn and Pisces.

Positive Aspects: Unconditional love on all levels of consciousness.

Negative Aspects: Rejection, manipulation and lack of love.

Physical vulnerabilities are the womb and the heart.

The frequency of the colour pink can affect you on a love vibration. Pink is for love – not just any kind of love but for unconditional love – love without conditions. Pink helps you to love yourself rather than be dependant upon others to love you. Because pink has the hidden colours of red and white within, it can convey the same healing qualities as those colours. |

Table 2 *continued*

White	White is not linked to any specific star sign.
	Positive Aspects: Having clear vision to see things more clearly, seeing the whole picture.
	Negative Aspects: Unshed tears through blocked vision and a need to release toxins.
	Physical vulnerabilities can be linked to anything because white carries all colours.
	White is a reflection of light that vibrates at different frequencies. It is these frequencies of light that create all colour. White carries all of the colours and can bring light into a situation where there has been too much darkness. White helps you to clear your vision on your pathway in life. Because white has all the hidden colours within, it can convey the same healing qualities of all colours. White also reflects light particles of colour energy.
Black	Black is not linked to any specific star sign.
	Positive Aspects: Deep emotional healing powers.
	Negative Aspects: Depression, apathy and fear of the darkness.
	Physical vulnerabilities can be linked to very deep issues.
	Black is a darkness, the absence of light. Even though black looks dark and colourless it does actually absorb all light particles, thus it is not as dark as it seems. Black has all the hidden colours within but on a very deep level. Because black has all the hidden colours within, it can convey on a very deep level all the healing qualities of all colours.

Table 2 *continued*

Brown	Brown is not linked to any specific star sign.
	Positive Aspects: Earth-grounding and Earth healer.
	Negative Aspects: Lack of balance, harmony and direction.
	The frequency of the colour brown is very good for grounding you before or after meditation or even in general. Brown can help you to balance your chakras on a very deep level of consciousness. Because brown has the hidden colours of all the complementary colours within, it can convey the same healing qualities of those colours.

The positive aspects of your choice of colour or the colours you are attracted to indicate the potential linked to the colours in your aura and the negative aspects are linked to the karma and lessons in your life. Negative karma can create an imbalance and dis-harmony on all levels of consciousness as you work through the many lessons in your life. By using the colours in your aura on a positive level it can heal the balance and dis-harmony that the karma or lessons might have created.

Look out for the many hidden colours that come together to create other colours, like red and blue coming together as violet, or yellow and blue coming together as green, or red and yellow coming together as orange.

Pastel Shades are linked to the many hues of different colours. Simply by adding a small proportion of a darker hue of any colour to white, you can create a pastel shade of your choice. See the colour wheel diagrams opposite pages 24 and 25. The pastel shades are on the outer edges of the wheels and they are intensified, which means they are more powerful because they have white running through them and white carries the light of all colours. This also means that they have more intensified traits and aspects, both positive and negative.

If your choice of colour appears to consist mainly of one colour then you may be in need of its complementary colour, crystals and sound frequency. See the separate chapters on crystals and sound.

Diagram Three (opposite page 24) illustrates the complementary colours of a traditional colour wheel. Diagram Four (opposite page 25) illustrates the complementary colours of the geometrical colour wheel. They are called complementary simply because they can actually complement each other. Some colours are magnetic in energy and some colours are electric in energy. Ideally you need both magnetic and electric colours to maintain a healthy balance. If your choice of colour is mainly made up of hues of Red (which are magnetic), then take a look at the hues of Jade/Turquoise and Sapphire (which are electric) because their qualities may help you to maintain a balance and vice versa. If your choice is mainly made up of hues of Orange (which are magnetic), then take a look at the hues of Royal Blue and Indigo (which are electric) because their qualities may help you to maintain a balance and vice versa. If your choice is mainly made up of hues of Yellow and Gold (which are magnetic), then take a look at the hues of Violet (which are electric) because their qualities may help you to maintain a balance and vice versa. If your choice is mainly made up of hues of Greens (which are neutral with magnetic and electric energies), then take a look at the hues of Magenta (which are also neutral with magnetic and electric energies) because their qualities may help you to maintain a balance and vice versa. The diagrams of the colour wheels also indicate how the pastel shades are linked to each hue of colour. The colour wheels also show one of the many healing frequencies of sound that can help to put you back into balance. Singers often go through a daily exercise of singing Doh, Ray, Me, Fah, Soh, Lah, Te, Doh. I wonder if they realise that they may actually be singing or chanting the balance of colour?

3

Magnet Therapy

Magnet Therapy is one of nature's most natural, alternative, non-toxic healing therapies, which can be dated back to the Egyptians, the Chinese and many far Eastern countries. Ancient texts have described how magnets were used for their therapeutic healing qualities. In ancient Vedic religious scriptures of India there are references that seem to indicate that magnets were used 5,000 years ago to treat diseases. It is thought that Cleopatra wore magnets to retain her youth, beauty and her health. Philosophers such as Aristotle and Plato talked about the therapeutic healing properties of magnets. Doctors in the Middle Ages used magnets to draw disease out of the body.

Magnet Therapy appears to work on a cellular level by enhancing the body's cells. The energy within us forms part of the electromagnetic field of which we are made up. Without a magnetic field we would soon fall ill and thus lose our balance because disease or illness would set in.

The planet Earth is one big magnet. The Earth has a North and South Pole and as the Earth spins it creates a magnetic field around it of both polarities (negative & positive). Electrons (magnetic energy) from the North Pole spin left (counter clockwise) generating negative magnetic energy, while electrons from the South Pole spin right (clockwise) generating positive magnetic energy. These polarities form a natural balance of positive and negative charges of energy. The South Pole is positive in frequency and the North Pole is negative in frequency. The same thing occurs with magnets. There are two sides to a magnet – north which generates negative magnetic energy and south which generates positive magnetic energy. To find out which side of a magnet is north and which side is south you will either need a pre-marked magnet or a compass. Magnets that are pre-marked north or south can be misleading because there are two contradictory systems for pre-marking magnets. In industry and navigation the north and south sides to a magnet are reversed because they use the direction of a compass to find the north when, in fact, a compass does *not* point north. Contrary to what most people believe, a compass points south, not north. Generally the coloured part of the compass needle indicates the direction in which the magnetic North Pole lies. The letter 'N' is often marked on that side as well. Although the coloured part of the needle indicates the geographic North Pole, its position is really oriented towards the magnetic Southern Pole. This has caused much confusion in the past so scientists now use the term 'North-seeking Pole' to designate what we commonly refer to as the south side of a magnet. Because opposites attract, it is actually the south side of a magnet that points to the Earth's magnetic North Pole. The 'North-seeking Pole' is the south side of a magnet and the 'South-seeking Pole' is the north side of a magnet. To find out which is the north or south side of a magnet using a compass, find the needle on the compass which points to the Earth's magnetic north, this will also point to the north side of your magnet. Although this might seem somewhat confusing, it is necessary to make it very clear when using magnets for alternative healing. Most magnet therapists usually keep to using the north side of the magnets because it is the north side that helps to maintain a healthy balance. The north side of a magnet is renowned for its relaxing properties whereas the south side of a magnet is renowned for its stimulating properties. Not all magnets have a north-facing side and a south-facing side. There are magnets called 'bi-polar magnets' which have positive and negative magnetic energy on the same side. Bi-polar magnets are usually used in industry or for fridge-magnets rather than for alternative healing.

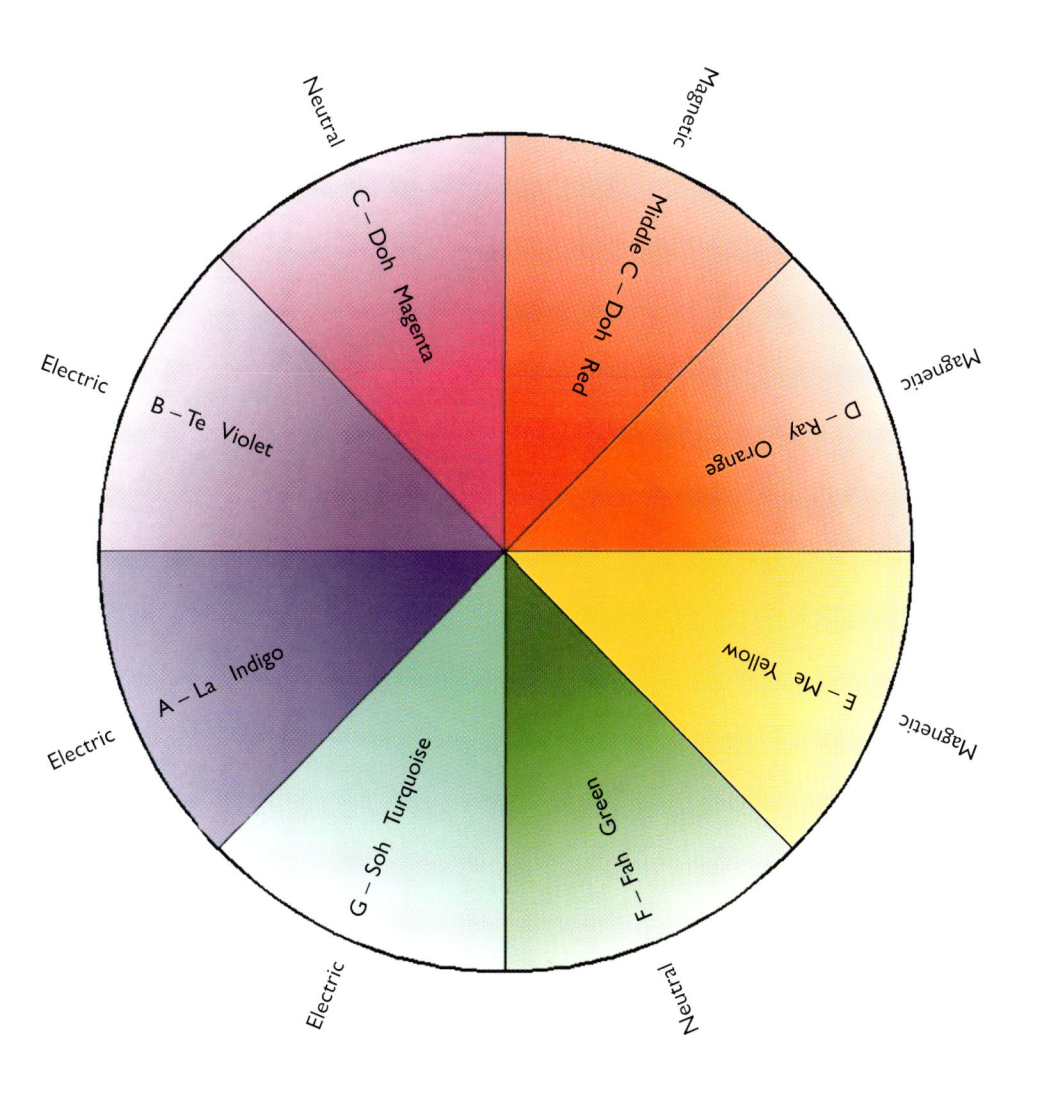

Diagram 3 The Traditional Complementary Colour Wheel with Sound.

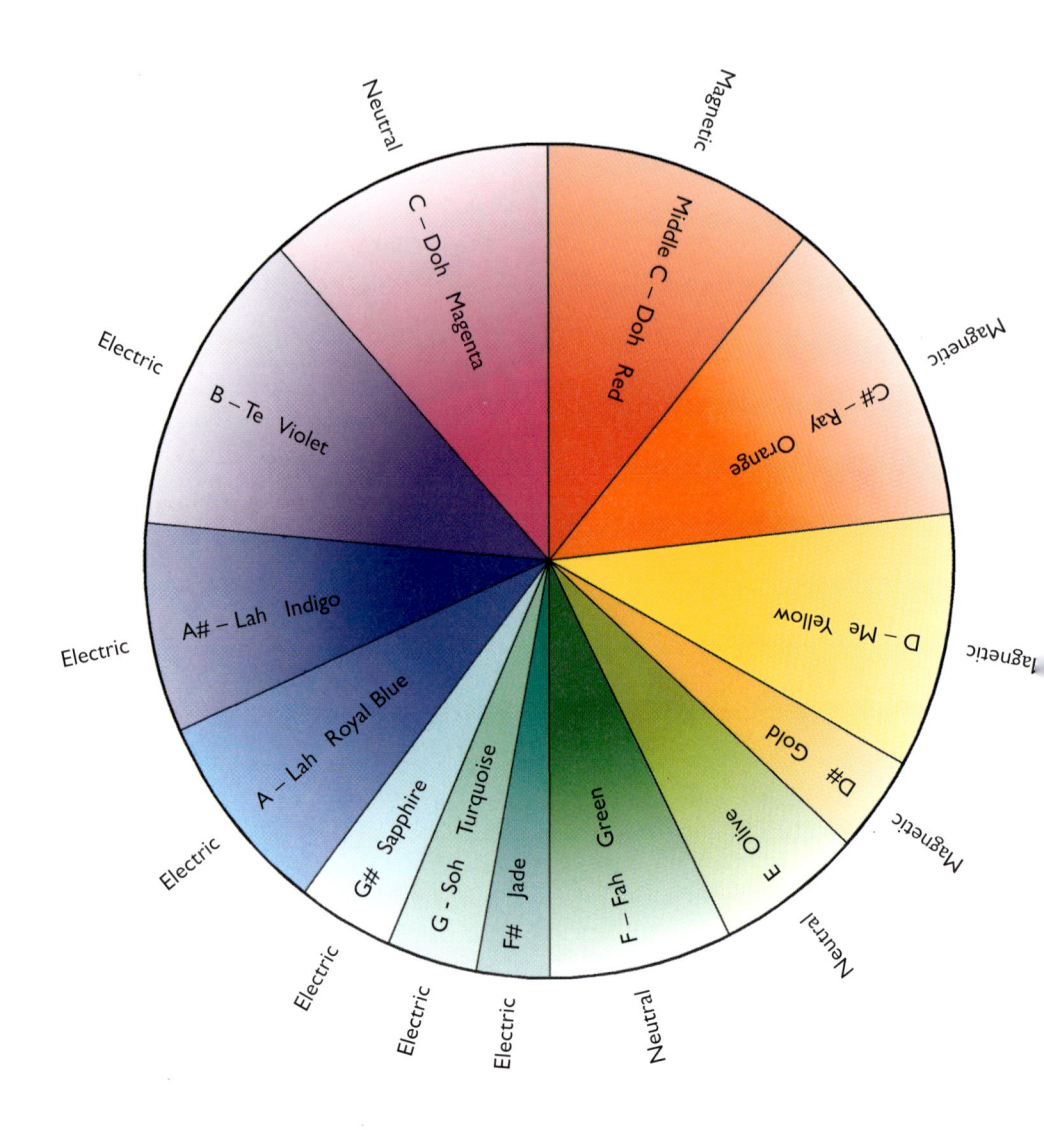

Diagram 4 The Geometrical Complementary Colour Wheel with Sound.

The Earth's natural electromagnetic field has been diminishing over the last few hundred years and, apart from industrial chemical pollution, one of the many reasons for this could be linked to modern man having introduced a form of energy that has contributed largely to the effect on the Earth's natural electromagnetic energy. This energy is called 'electricity'. Electricity increases the positive magnetic energy which can have an effect on our own electromagnetic field in the same way as the Earth's by making it weak and vulnerable. If we are exposed to too much electricity for too long (or in fact any pollution) we can lose our natural electromagnetic balance and become weak. When our electromagnetic field is weak it can reduce cell growth which is important to our immune system as well as our nervous system. Nervous stress can kill hormones that are vital to our immune system.

Remaining in good health is a constant battle of balancing our energies – positive and negative. Positive magnetic energy can be caused by external pollution (including electricity), food allergies, excessive alcohol, caffeine and poor diet. It is the positive magnetic energy that is responsible for attacking the balance, causing disharmony and disease. By administering Magnet Therapy most disease or illness can be put back into balance safely and naturally by re-balancing magnetic currents in and around the physical body. Magnet Therapy can also accelerate the healing of wounds and alleviate pain during and after operations.

Electromagnetic field devices are often used in hospitals by doctors and physiotherapists to help ease paralysis, neuromotor disorders and problems related to muscles, rheumatism and arthritis and to accelerate the healing of fractures.

Magnet Therapy can be applied in numerous ways. Jewelry can be made out of magnets and worn. Magnetic inner-soles can be purchased and worn inside shoes. There are magnet therapists who place magnets directly onto the skin on specific parts of the body known as meridians or acupuncture points. Meridians are invisible channels or energy lines that run through the physical body. Acupuncture is an ancient Chinese approach to alternative healing, whereby sterile needles are inserted into the skin at specific points that are located along the meridian lines. Magnets can also be placed into the bath or even in drinking water, procedures which can be very powerful as water is a very good conductor for energy.

Magnets have been known to lose their magnetism on a gradual basis thus making them weaker but this is usually a very slow process over many years. It is the same process that the Earth herself has been going through and has always gone through. The Earth appears to release or lose electromagnetic energy and then seemingly gets it back again.

Please note that it is not advised that you place magnets near or too close to electrical appliances that rely on a memory database because magnets can erase collective memory data. Magnets can also erase credit cards, so it is advisable that you keep them well away from your purse or wallet! People who have a pace-maker should also avoid being too close to magnets.

4

Crystals and their Healing Potential

Crystals are minerals that are made up of solidified substances in definite geometrical forms. Some crystals are formed when lava from the Earth's core pushes its way up through the rock and slowly cools down. Some are the result of the fusion of minerals on the Earth's surface and others can be formed when minerals are placed under great pressure and exposed to great heat within the Earth's crust.

Crystals can be traced back to the dawning of civilisation. Ancient texts (including the Bible) refer to crystals and their uses. The ancient Egyptians, Chinese, Sumerians, Mayans, Aztecs, American Indians and many other cultures used crystals not only for their healing properties but they were often worn by high priests and high priestesses and people who held some form of spiritual power. They were worn for protection, spiritual power and for their healing properties.

Crystals were (and still are) known for their powerful healing potential and magical properties. Crystals can also heal on a cellular level like the magnets but crystals are slightly different from magnets in their vibratory rates. Like colours, crystals vibrate at different frequencies and these vibrational frequencies are often in resonance with the body's chakra system. This is how crystals can work with colour to heal the body and put back its natural balance on all levels of consciousness. Each crystal is unique and can heal in its own way, carrying its own healing vibration. Crystals can heal by putting back the balance within each chakra. The chakras feed from the vibrational energy within the crystal. This energy is then fed through the relevant chakra and its natural balance can be attained. Crystals are also used for purposes other than healing such as teaching or channelling. Table 3 lists some of the many crystals that are linked to the new geometrical chakra system. These crystals can help to maintain a healthy balance physically, emotionally, mentally and spiritually

Like magnets crystals can be applied in numerous ways. Jewelry in many forms can be made from crystals and is a very popular way of naturally using the therapeutic healing energy within them. Crystals can be sewn onto clothing, incorporated in architectural buildings and sculptures, crushed into powder for make-up or artwork, or used as tools. Diamonds are well known as cutting tools and tools such as a diamond-tipped drill used by dentists. Crystal healers often use crystal wands for healing. There are numerous ways in which crystal healers work but most of them use the layout system whereby the healer uses his/her intuition and knowledge to select crystals to lay on or around the physical body.

There are many books that you can purchase on crystals and their uses for healing purposes. There are also many hundreds of crystals that can be purchased. When you buy crystals, for whatever reasons, you should feel magnetically drawn to them. Crystals have electromagnetic energies that can resonate with you. Perhaps you are drawn to certain crystals for their colour or their magnetic pull. All that you are drawn to is part of who you are and what you need to work on within yourself.

Crystals and their Healing Potential

Table 3 Crystals linked to the new geometrical chakra system

Red **The Base Chakra**
Obsidian is magnetic and keeps you grounded.
Ruby improves the blood circulation.
Haematite aids blood disorders such as anaemia.
Carnelian improves sexual drive and passion.
Garnet improves stamina and endurance.
Pyrite energises the magnetic field.
Bloodstone improves the blood circulation.

The frequencies of crystals that work with the Base Chakra are effective for stimulating underactive conditions. These crystals are good for impotence and passion. They help energise the blood and blood circulation. They are also beneficial to lower back problems.

Orange **The Sacral Chakra**
Carnelian calms shock, trauma and stress.
Topaz calms anxiety and the bladder.
Jasper activates grounding energy.
Moonstone relieves menstrual pain.

The frequencies of crystals that work with the Sacral Chakra are effective for shock, fear and trauma. These crystals are also effective on the spleen, hormones and lower abdomen.

Yellow **The Solar Plexus Chakra**
Citrine calms nervous stress and aids knowledge.
Yellow Jade helps to clear mental blockages.
Yellow Jasper aids the immune system.
Yellow Calcite improves kidney function.

The frequencies of crystals that work with the Solar Plexus Chakra are effective for nervous fear. The skin is often affected through nervous fear and these crystals carry beneficial healing frequencies for this. These crystals can also be beneficial to the liver, kidneys, stomach, gall bladder and digestive tract, all of which are affected by nervous stress and anxiety.

Table 3 *continued*

Gold	**The Golden Star Chakra**
	Amber gives you courage and improves memory.
	Smoky Quartz eases fear linked to stress.
	Tiger's Eye awakens spirituality through gut feelings.
	Chrysocolla increases spiritual inspiration.
	The frequencies of crystals that work with the Golden Star Chakra are effective for deep fear, shock and trauma, which in turn affect the adrenals and the nervous system. Therefore, these crystals are effective for the kidneys, liver, bladder, stomach and digestive tract.
Olive	**The Lower Heart Chakra**
	Green Jasper clears emotional blockages.
	Peridot calms emotional confusion and phobias.
	The frequencies of crystals that work with the Lower Heart Chakra are effective for emotional shock, trauma and stress, which put a strain on the heart and lungs. Therefore, these crystals are effective for the heart and lungs.
Emerald Green	**The Heart Chakra**
	Aventurine aids in detoxifying heart and lungs.
	Beryl/Aquamarine helps to maintain polarity of balance.
	Chrysoprase can lift emotional depression.
	Moonstone improves love in relationships.
	Rose Quartz helps one to love the self.
	Moss Agate strengthens the emotions.
	The frequencies of crystals that work with the Heart Chakra are effective for all kinds of emotional turmoil. These crystals are cleansing crystals that clean up the emotions by bringing in balance and harmony by cleansing your own space. Therefore, these crystals are effective for the heart, lungs and blood pressure. Whether high or low these crystals can help to balance blood pressure.

Table 3 *continued*

Jade	**The Upper Heart Chakra**
	Malachite breaks old negative patterns.
	Jade encourages emotional wisdom.
	Green Fluorite strengthens the immune system.
	Tourmaline helps build chest and lung immunity.
	The frequencies of crystals that work with the Upper Heart Chakra are effective for the immune system.
Turquoise	**The Throat Chakra**
	Turquoise aids in overcoming communication difficulties.
	Blue Jade encourages communication.
	Blue Lace Agate calms and brings peace.
	The frequencies of crystals that work with the Throat Chakra are effective for the breath and the vocal chords. Therefore, these crystals calm the breathing and, thus, are effective for asthma, chest infections and bronchitis.
Sapphire	**The Spiritual Protection Chakra**
	Sapphire protects against spiritual fears.
	Aquamarine/Beryl aids psychic awareness.
	Celestite brings in angelic protection.
	Amazonite brings in spiritual truth and trust.
	The frequencies of crystals that work with the Spiritual Protection Chakra are effective for calming the breath linked to spiritual fears. Therefore, these crystals calm palpitations of the heart.

Table 3 *continued*

Royal Blue **The Cerebellum Chakra**
Lapis Lazuli activates and protects spirituality.
Azurite activates the subconscious mind.
Labradorite helps inner balance.
Blue Chalcedony helps you to remember your dreams.

The frequencies of crystals that work with the Cerebellum Chakra are effective for easing problems with ears, eyes, nose, throat and also teeth, as well as the brain.

Indigo **The Third Eye Chakra**
Sodalite aids in overcoming memory loss.
Sugilite aids with eliminating negative thought patterns.
Amethyst calms the mind when too much energy is within the head.
Tiger's Eye opens and protects the third eye in meditation.
Opal brings clear vision in meditation.

The frequencies of crystals that work with the Third Eye Chakra are effective for easing problems with ears, eyes, nose, throat and also teeth. These crystals can also help to ease poor memory, clumsiness and vertigo.

Violet **The Crown Chakra**
Amethyst heals on all levels of consciousness.
Purple Fluorite links spiritual and physical energies together.
Moonstone helps disperse negative energy and thought when meditating with it in the full moon.
White Onyx aids in clearing the mind of worries and stress.

The frequencies of crystals that work with the Crown Chakra are effective for any head condition such as headaches, migraines, insomnia and stress brought on through worry.

Crystals and their Healing Potential

Table 3 *continued*

Magenta	***An Astral Chakra*** Rose Quartz stimulates unconditional love. Clear Quartz activates clear thought and clear vision. Selenite purifies negative fears. Celestite links you into the fairies and the angelic realms. Diamonds are linked to purity, clarity of vision and spiritual light. *The frequencies of crystals that work with the Astral Chakras are effective for putting back the love that is lost through a divine healing. When you cannot find love on the physical level then these crystals can help you link in with the divine energy to bring down love from Heaven to Earth.*
White	White is linked to the White Light that enters the Crown through the Astral Chakras. It is a healing light which healers channel through to use with their healing. White carries all the colours and can bring light into situations where there has been too much darkness. White clears the vision on all levels of consciousness. Clear Quartz clears and purifies on all levels of consciousness. Herkimer Diamond activates spiritual power and light. *The frequencies of crystals that work with the White Light are effective anywhere on any level of consciousness.*

5

Healing with Sound

Sound is made up of vibrational frequencies. Colour is light that is vibrating at different frequencies, therefore, that too is linked to sound. Crystals, whether coloured or clear, resonate to both sound and colour frequencies, therefore, they too are linked to sound.

Sound vibrations can release a chemical called melatonin that creates a luminescent light from the fontanelle. It is the melatonin, which gives the impression of a halo around the head. Melatonin seems to respond to sound and light (colour) frequency.

Sound works on a cellular level by means of waveforms. Waveforms are patterns of energy (normally invisible to the naked eye). Waveforms can be measured on scientific apparatus in the forms of assorted lines – some wavy, some straight, some staggered or even broken. Sound waveforms can be measured in wavelengths of speed ranging from very slow frequencies to very fast frequencies. For instance, red can be measured as being slow in waveform whereas blue can be measured as being fast in waveform.

Sound penetrates the body by entering every cell as a vibrational frequency. Cells are constantly being produced and they form the basic units of the human body. Each cell contains a nucleus and protoplasm, which is the essential building material for the body. If the body is out of balance then it is because the cells are not healthy or not being developed efficiently. Each cell divides to build up tissues and this all takes efficient vibratory movement within the body. A pure note or sound frequency produces vibratory waveforms of energy that can help develop healthy cells. A pure note or sound can be measured on most chromatic tuners that measure each note as being in perfect tune or perfect pitch. The waveforms or patterns from sound penetrate the body and help put back the balance and harmony with vibratory movement. If healthy cells are being developed then a healthy mind, body and spirit are being developed too.

Every virus or disease vibrates at a frequency that is unfamiliar to the physical body. This is why we feel ill and out of balance. The body tells us when we are not vibrating at the correct frequency or wavelength. Pure sound frequencies are not unfamiliar to the physical body and pure sound can help to re-balance each cell that has been put out of balance. Pure sound does this by re-programming each cell.

Frequencies of the physical body can be measured in kHz (kilohertz). When cells have been re-balanced or re-programmed they vibrate at a frequency that can be measured between 140 and 180 kHz. This is a healthy vibratory rate. People with dis-ease or imbalance emit wavelengths much higher in frequency, some reaching 400 to 500 kHz, which represents a vibratory imbalance.

Sound therapy can help to balance the chakra system as well as the auric field, which surrounds the physical body. Each chakra vibrates at a different colour frequency and each chakra vibrates at a different sound frequency. See Diagram One and Diagram Two opposite pages 8 and 9 These diagrams indicate the old traditional chakra system and the new geometrical chakra system and how they both work with sound and colour vibration. Both can be used and both can be equally beneficial. It is good to have different systems because each individual's needs are different.

The following paragraphs have been taken from *Starchild* Chapter Three.

The chakras enjoy pure sound frequencies and can appear to be stimulated or relaxed by certain tones. How often are you moved only by certain pieces of music or certain chords, only at certain times of your life? When you enjoy listening to music you send out the frequency of unconditional love which raises the vibration within your aura. Even heavy metal bands can have this same effect if this is the music you really enjoy. Once unconditional love is sent out into your aura the chakras respond by accepting and resonating with the healing vibration of sound. How many of you actually relieve the stress of a hard day by putting on your favourite piece of music? Never underestimate the healing power of sound. You may be aware on a conscious level of music therapeutically making you feel better but on a subconscious level your chakras are being put back into balance and are, therefore, being healed.

Listed below are the middle octave notes of a keyboard and how the notes relate to the old traditional chakra system and the new geometrical awakening chakra system.

The old traditional chakra system does not include the sharps and this is what makes the two systems slightly different.

The old traditional chakra system:

Middle	C	=	Red	Doh
	D	=	Orange	Ray
	E	=	Yellow	Me
	F	=	Green	Fah
	G	=	Blue	Soh
	A	=	Indigo	Lah
	B	=	Violet	Te

Healing with Sound

The new geometrical chakra system:

Middle C	=	Red	G	=	Turquoise
C#	=	Orange	G#	=	Sapphire
D	=	Yellow	A	=	Royal Blue
D#	=	Gold	A#	=	Indigo
E	=	Olive	B	=	Violet
F	=	Green	C	=	Magenta
F#	=	Jade			

The thirteenth chakra/sound frequency is the beginning of a whole new octave.

Whether using the old traditional system or the new geometrical system the benefits can be equally the same. If you play the individual notes of either system on a keyboard it can help you to put back the balance of each chakra. You may find that your favourite sound frequencies resonate with your favourite colours.

Sound is one of the most powerful tools that we have for healing. Sound therapy is often felt by each individual in an area where it is needed. Like colour, sound can be used and felt in different ways. The sound of music can be healing but what about sound itself? Sound can be created from crystal bowls. Crystal bowls come in various sizes and different sizes create different notes. A specialist in this field will know which note is needed and play the relevant bowl or bowls. Special tuning forks can be purchased for healing. The tuning forks can be purchased in any note. Once a tuning fork is struck it creates a sound frequency and the note from each tuning fork can be gently placed into the relevant chakra. Sound does not have to be kept strictly to the chakra system. Remember, sound frequencies can enter the whole body by entering each cell as a vibrational frequency.

Everything around you (whether natural or man-made) is made up of vibrational frequencies, therefore, everything is linked to sound. Everything vibrates at a frequency that creates its own sound, most of which cannot be picked up by the human ear. It is the speed of vibration that holds things together or gives the impression that they are of solid form.

Sound can vibrate at a positive or negative frequency. Music to one person's ears may not be music to another's – it depends on the individual's needs at that time.

Positive and negative sound vibration is everywhere. Positive and negative sound vibration also goes out from the Earth into the universe. It is in the universe where all energies are balanced, including sound.

Positive sound vibrations are pure tones or notes that come from perfectly tuned instruments, crystal bowls, tuning forks or voice patterning such as perfect pitch singing, toning or chanting. Negative sound vibrations are not pure sounds. These notes can come from instruments or voice patterning that is out of tune. Negative voice patterning can produce short sharp vibrations that often appear to look fragmented or out of tune. When you hear somebody scream in fear it can produce short sharp sound waves within their voice patterning (their voice often appears to be breaking up) but because different people feel fear in different ways, the opposite might occur. For instance, sometimes the brain temporarily erases the fear and can leave the person looking calm and sometimes speechless, which can create a false impression of the sound waves being emitted from the person's voice patterning. This second form of fear will almost certainly come out eventually and could possibly have similar effects to the first. So, fear can be linked to both positive and negative sound waves. Fear felt in the physical body can affect the aura. As the negative sound waves penetrate the aura they can create gaps in the colours, which are called auric gaps.

Positive and negative sound vibrations can also relate to people's voices.

Negative people often have slow droning voices that can be quite draining on others. A child (or an adult) can sometimes whine for something, which is also linked to negative sound frequencies and they, too, can be quite draining. Positive people are bubbly and quite uplifting.

Healing with Sound

There are several ways you can put back your own healing balance and harmony with sound therapy.

Swimming with the dolphins can have a very powerful effect on those in need of healing. Ironically, I wrote this chapter the day that I swam with the dolphins. I thought that I was going to have a day off from writing but I was wrong because this day was very relevant to this chapter. There was something that wasn't quite clear in my mind with regard to how the dolphins heal through communication. As I entered the water, I was approached by two large male dolphins that circled me. As one surfaced he looked me right in the eye and communication began instantly. Initially it spooked me because he was reading my thought patterns – he knew what I needed to know for this chapter and gave me the information through telepathy. I watched the pair of males demonstrating their technique with other people who were in the water with us. The following information comes from the dolphins themselves. Dolphins love healing and they use the power of unconditional love to create high vibrational frequencies that they can adapt to suit each individual's needs. Dolphins create sounds that human beings would find hard to match. The clicking and squeaks you hear form part of their radar. A dolphin's radar is made up of pure sound and this is why dolphins are renowned for healing people. The physical body is seventy percent water and that is why the body is very receptive to healing vibrational energy through water. In the water sound vibration penetrates the physical body on a cellular level, thus putting back the body's balance through vibrational movement of the cells and their growth. Dolphins are aware of our cellular structure and know when we are out of balance or ill. They pick up our imbalance or illness by using their extra sensitive radar perception. They appear to make more sounds around those who are in need of healing. These sounds can help to put back each individual's balance on a physical, emotional, mental and spiritual level by touching and resonating through each person's entire being. The dolphins could teach us so much about sound healing through the power of unconditional love. Dolphins (like other cetaceans) use sound through radar to communicate and because water is a very good conductor for carrying sound frequencies the dolphins' messages can be picked up for many miles.

If you are not fortunate enough to be able to swim with the dolphins then try the next best thing – listening to dolphins' music. Dolphin sounds can be very therapeutic for you especially whilst relaxing in the bath.

Sharks can pick up the vibration of fear through the water for many miles and because some of them are predators they will home in with their radar on the negative vibrational sound waves and quite often attack.

Humans also send out constant sound frequencies (not normally heard by the human ear). Whether in or out of water, both positive and negative energies are being emitted from the human body (mostly on a subconscious level). When humans feel full of fear they produce adrenalin, which sends out a negative sound frequency into the aura, thus upsetting or damaging the colours within it. This damage can be the cause of imbalance on all levels of consciousness and if this energy is sent through the water it can be amplified. For instance, if you go under the water and make a verbal sound, it might sound muffled but it is amplified. Equally, if humans feel full of love and are well balanced they produce a chemical called melatonin, which sends out a gentle, calm sound frequency into the aura. Sound frequencies through the water are amplified because water is a good conductor for vibrational sound waves, as it is for the vibrational waves of colour, magnets and crystals.

Singing in the bath or the shower can help to tune up your chakra system. You can sing or hum the sounds you need to heal yourself but remember, your singing or humming may not benefit another's needs so, keep your own singing or humming out of earshot of those who are not resonating with it. Simple sound exercises in the bath or shower can

Healing with Sound

be sung and the relevant colours visualised in the chakra areas. Try singing and visualising the following:

Doh	Red	The Base Chakra
Ray	Orange	The Sacral Chakra
Me	Yellow	The Solar Plexus Chakra
Fah	Green	The Heart Chakra
Soh	Blue	The Throat Chakra
Lah	Indigo	The Third Eye Chakra
Te	Violet	The Crown Chakra
Doh	Magenta	The Astral Chakra

Sound therapists work in various ways. Some sound therapists use the pure tone in their voice to help restore balance whilst others use the pure crystalline sound that permeates through crystal bowls. Other methods used are Tibetan bowls and tuning forks. Some sound therapists suggest that you chant yourself back into balance. There are many different chants and this is good because each individual's needs are different. You may have come across some of the following chants linked to the old traditional chakra system. Try chanting them all to see which one you are comfortable with.

Base	UH	LAM	AY	DOH
Sacral	OOO	VAM	EEE	RAY
Solar Plexus	OH	RAM	OM	ME
Heart	AH	YAM	AH	FAH
Throat	EYE	HAM	EYE	SOH
Third Eye	AY	KSHAM	OWE	LAH
Crown	EEE	OM	YOO	TE

Group chanting can be very powerful because this can create overtones that are extremely beneficial healing vibrations. Overtones in chanting are sound vibrations that are often heard long after the chanting has stopped. Overtones in music are a subtle extra quality of other harmonics. I remember chanting in a large group once and its powerful vibrational energy brought down the entire cornice in the room.

Laughter is a sound frequency unique to each individual's needs. One person's laughter can be another person's pain but your own laughter can be very healing for you. When you laugh (even nervously) you release endorphins, which are derived from a substance within the pituitary gland called beta-lipotropin. These endorphins are your body's own natural pain killers which can ease the overwork of the adrenals in a crisis situation.

Tibetan chanting (or any kind of chanting) is very powerful for healing with sound and there is a wide variety of such music that can be purchased. The OM sound is linked to the sound vibration of the universe itself and, therefore, can help you to link in to the universe. Equally, the North American Indians, and many other tribes such as the Aborigines and the ancient Dogon tribes of Africa, have always had different ceremonies whereby they used (and still do use) chants and chanting. This chanting apparently took (and still does take) them into higher levels of consciousness and also into different dimensions of reality.

Tibetan chanting (or any kind of chanting) often uses 'Mantras'. A Mantra is where you repeat a verse or several lines of words (often seen written in Sanskrit). Mantras should never be underestimated because this form of chanting is very powerful. Mantras can help you to relax at a deep level of consciousness taking you into a meditative state. The sound waves released by repeating Mantras can help to balance and heal your physical, emotional and spiritual being.

Below are some of the many Mantras that you may have come across. Try sitting in a quiet room where you will not be disturbed and repeat a Mantra that feels comfortable with you.

The Krishna Mantra

Hare Krishna, Hare Krishna – Krishna, Krishna, Hare Hare.
Rama Rama, Hara Hara – Hare Krishna, Hare Krishna.
Krishna, Krishna, Hare Hare.

Rama Rama, Hara Hara Hare Krishna, Hare Krishna, Krishna.
*(Hail to Krishna, Hail to Krishna, Krishna Krishna, Hail Hail.
Hail to Rama, Hail to Rama, Rama Rama, Hail Hail.)*

The Great Peace Mantra
Om Shanti, Shanti, Shanti.
(Om Peace, Peace, Peace.)

Hebrew Mantra
Shalom – Shalom – Shalom – Shalom – Shalom – Shalom.
(Peace – Peace – Peace – Peace – Peace – Peace.)

Om Mane Padme Hum
Aa-oo-m Mah-nee-Pad-may Hoom.
(Om Jewel in the Lotus hum.)

Gayatri Mantra
Om Bhoor – Bhuvaha Swaha – Tat Savitur – Vareniyam – Bhargo Devasya – Dheemahi Dhiyo – Yo Naha – Prachodayat.
(O God, you are the giver of life, the remover of pain and sorrow, the bestower of happiness. O Creator of the universe, may we receive your supreme sin-destroying light. May you guide our intellect in the right direction.)

Islamic Mantra
Qol huan – Allahu – achad – Allahu – as-samad
Lam yalid – wa-lam – yulad – wa-lam – yaqun – lahu – kuwan – achad.
(He is Allah the One. Allah the eternal besought of all. He begetteth not nor was begotten and there is none comparable him.)

Egyptian Mantra
Nuk-Puk-Nuk – Au-u – Ur-se-ur – Au-u.
(I am the great One, son of the great One, I am.)

Christian Mantra
Kyrie – Eleison – Christe – Eleison.
(Lord have mercy upon us – Christ have mercy upon us.)

Listening to music that you enjoy can help to harmonise your balance but listening to the music being played in musical concerts in a large hall can create an incredible vibration of energy. As each individual expresses love and passion for music in different ways they give off the power of unconditional love from the heart. This amplifies the sound vibration even more and it is extremely therapeutic on a healing level. Sometimes this energy reaches such an incredible 'high' that people begin to feel overwhelmed by it all and begin to cry or stand up and clap. Crying heals by releasing blocked energy, whereas clapping (because it is not pure sound – clapping is out of tune) breaks down the power of the sound frequency and thus the healing energy from it ceases. Many people who go to concerts on a regular basis will find that things are changing and people are beginning to respond to this powerful healing frequency of sound by gently waving their hands instead.

Sound can have very profound effects on many different people in many different ways. Sound is around you and runs through you all day, every day because you are made up of vibrational energy and vibrational energy is sound. You are sound.

When you are ill or become out of balance, the sound frequencies of which you are made are 'out of tune' and dis-harmony sets in. This dis-harmony is linked to sound pollution.

Sound pollution can cause dis-harmony because sound pollution is not pure sound, it is negative in frequency and, therefore, unfamiliar to the human body.

Sound pollution is caused by very low frequency waves being emitted from overhead cables/wires, electrical equipment, office equipment, televisions, computers and the list goes on and on. Although sound pollution is negative in frequency to the human body, these appliances actually emit positive magnetic energy. All electrical equipment creates unseen atmospheric sound pollution, which in turn can cause magnetic field deficiency in and around the human body.

Some scientists have been researching for many years the theory that most cancers are probably linked to radiation given off from positive magnetic energy.

Some countries have actually invented a stun gun that fires low frequency sound waves at people in order to control crowds in a riot situation. They believe this stun gun to be less dangerous than their previously used pepper balls or various sprays. This stun gun is actually firing ammunition that causes disease. Whether the inventors realise it or not, negative sound rays such as these are far more dangerous to use on a long-term basis. Negative sound frequencies destroy the astral layers of the aura, thus damaging the chakras and the organs they are linked to.

Very low frequency waves can cause stress, which in turn affects the nervous system, immune system and hormone production. Low frequency waves cause fatigue, nausea, headaches, irritability, memory loss, heart conditions, miscarriages and the list goes on and on.

On a scientific level, when you have been exposed to too much electrical pollution it increases the level of a chemical in the blood called serotonin that results in irritability and mood-swings. It is the resulting irritability and mood-swings that can destroy families, marriages and relationships. This is why sound pollution can reach a dangerous level of destruction! The more electrical appliances you have within your home or office the more you run the risk of emotional imbalance, dis-harmony and destruction.

Sound pollution in the home can be emitted by electrical equipment (even if it is switched off) that releases positive magnetic energy. These positive magnetic energies build up into pockets of energy within your home, which have the opposite effect on the human body on all levels of consciousness - negative. This might sound confusing and even contradictory but it is linked to opposites attracting to each other as with magnets, a north magnet will attract a south magnet and vice-versa. To prevent any more confusion, from now on I shall refer to this positive magnetic energy as negative energy. When you have negative energy within your home it can also make you negative and those with whom you share your home too.

Negative energy can bring out the negative labels linked to the colours in your aura and also those who live with you. Negative energy can deplete your physical energy. This is why, when you sometimes watch the television for too long you become lethargic and lazy.

A microwave oven use electromagnetic waves to heat and cook foods. A microwave oven uses microwaves that are in the range of radio waves similar to those used in radar and satellite communications. When radio waves (such as the ones used in microwave ovens) are concentrated in a confined space such as a microwave with food in it, they heat the moisture within food, which makes it cook. It is the vibrational waves that produce the heat to make the food cook. If you have to use microwaves for cooking then try singing or chanting as you do so to create your own healing balance with pure sound.

To help eliminate sound pollution it is suggested that you chant or sing daily. Being inside a cave is a good way of protecting yourself against sound pollution but it is not always possible or practical. However, there are plenty of other ways to protect yourself and prevent sound pollution from affecting your life. If it is possible, try and empty your bedroom of all electrical appliances. A small bedside lamp should be adequate. Your bedroom is a resting area where you should sleep to restore your energy for the next day. If you have electrical appliances in the bedroom you may wake up more tired in the morning than when you went to bed! This is because the electrical appliances have slowly been draining you throughout the night. If it is possible, try to position your bed so that your head is facing north and your feet are pointing south. This can help with the energy flow around the physical body as you sleep. If this is not possible, then try to position your bed so that you actually get some natural sunlight in the morning. The sun neutralises harmful electromagnetic fields by balancing them with its own magnetic waves. Natural electromagnetic energy from the sun can help to eliminate sound pollution. You can surround electrical appliances with crystals such as amethyst or smoky quartz to help eliminate sound pollution but they will need to be regularly cleansed and recharged in the sunlight or the moonlight.

6

The Therapeutic Use of Aurora Bottles

The therapeutic use of Aurora bottles is very versatile. Although Aurora is a combination of four alternative therapies its versatility gives users the non-intrusive freedom of choice of whether they want to use just one, all or a combination of two or three different therapies.

In previous chapters I have mentioned the therapeutic use of the individual therapies that Aurora use – Colour, Magnets, Crystals and Sound. In this chapter I shall explain how all four alternative therapies can work together, each one enhancing the other.

The Aurora bottles are beautifully hand-decorated and their magnificent colours catch the eye of the beholder. It is this attraction to the bottles that draws each person to his/her needs. This initial attraction is also the first alternative therapy – Colour Healing.

The Aurora bottles have relevant coloured crystals attached to them around the neck. These can be removed or changed to suit the individual's needs. This is the second alternative therapy – Crystal Healing.

Aurora has designed a special base that fits the bottles. The base holds six north-facing magnets that can be removed to suit the individual's needs. This is the third alternative therapy – Magnet Healing.

The base is designed to hold a tuning fork that has a sound frequency relevant to the colour. The tuning forks can be removed or the note changed to suit the individual's needs. This is the fourth alternative therapy – Sound Healing.

With the versatility of Aurora users can either select a ready-made-up bottle of their choice or choose their own colour, crystals and sound. The bottles come with or without magnets, crystals or sound. The bottles can be made to suit each individual's needs because it is recognised that, like the bottles, each individual is unique and each individual's needs will, therefore, be different on all levels of consciousness.

The bottles are sold empty so that the user can fill them with base oil, aromatherapy oils for massage, or water for drinking purposes. If the coloured bottles are filled and placed into the base containing the magnets and the tuning fork all four alternative therapies can begin to work almost immediately. The magnets begin to magnify the effect of the healing powers within the crystals and also the vibration of each relevant sound and colour. When the tuning fork is struck the sound frequency of the note activates the vibrational energy of the contents within the bottle, which is then magnified by the energy in the colour, magnets and crystals. The contents within the bottle then become structured which can help to re-balance or re-programme the body's cells. Water and oils are very good conductors for carrying this healing energy created from colour, magnets, crystals and sound. Once the water has been drunk or the oils massaged into the physical body, the coloured, magnetic, crystal, sound energy within the water or the oils can start to work instantly through the physical body, thus putting back its natural magnetic balance. Structured water/oil is a safe and natural way of detoxifying and putting back the natural balance and harmony on all levels of consciousness.

When an Aurora bottle is filled with water and placed into the magnetic base it should be left for at least ten to fifteen minutes or at the discretion or intuition of the individual. The bottle can also be left in natural sunshine or even overnight in natural moonlight. The bottle should not be placed in the fridge with the magnets because electrical appliances have been known to drain the energy of the magnets. How often and how much one should drink this water is again, at the discretion or intuition of the individual. One must remember that anything can be good for you in moderation and two or three bottles of this water a day should be quite adequate and, for maximum benefit, the water should be drunk straight after pouring it.

Magnetised drinking water can be used in the bath, for cooking, added to natural fruit juices or an animal's drinking water or for houseplants. Natural squeezed lemon juice added to the magnetised water can aid with detoxification.

Approximately 70% of the human body is made up of water. The water that you drink can have an effect on your health. Tap water can have many added chemicals that are not natural to the human body but if you magnetise the water you can change its structure. Because you are mainly made up of water the body gets used to the water that you drink or even bath in, so when you change the water that you drink or bath in you are looking at changing your body, mind and spirit. A simple example is when you go on holiday. The water that you drink or bath in is different – the body begins to recognise the change and can often react. That tummy upset might not have been linked to something you ate but something you drank – a change in the water.

The effects of magnetised water:

1. The crystallisation within the water is increased.
2. The surface of the water changes.
3. Traces of nitrogen are expelled.
4. The PH value of the water changes.
5. The electrical conductivity of the water is enhanced.
6. The density of the water increases.
7. The water becomes softer.

When an Aurora bottle is filled with base oil or an aromatherapy oil and placed into the magnetic base it can be kept in the bottle for up to the expiry date of the oil itself. The magnetic base will increase the healing properties of the oils. How often and how much one should use this oil should be at the discretion of the individual or the individual's masseur.

Aurora Magnetic Crystal Sound Healing is a natural, non-intrusive way of re-charging your whole being on all levels of consciousness. Aurora can help to alleviate stress which is the main link to all imbalance or illness. Aurora can help you to gain relief from aches and pains, help you to sleep more deeply, build up your immune system, stimulate the circulation, expel toxins and improve the body's energy and strength.

Aurora complements other healing techniques and alternative therapies. Restructured water is natural and can be used with homoeopathy but some homoeopaths might not agree. If you are unsure about drinking structured water then check with your homoeopath.

It is advised that you keep your Aurora bottles (including the base) away from plug sockets and all electrical equipment because the frequencies from electrical appliances can drain the magnets.

Please note that it is advised that Aurora is an alternative therapy, therefore, no person should cease taking any medical treatments without first consulting their doctor. Aurora does not recommend this alternative therapy to children but like any alternative therapy, if a parent or parents intuitively feel that it would benefit their child or children then they do so at their own discretion.

As a precaution it is advised that people with serious heart conditions, those fitted with pace-makers, those suffering from mental illness and those suffering from epilepsy or convulsions should avoid using magnets. The reason for this is because the natural electromagnetic energy within the magnets can interfere with unnatural or unusual electrical impulses. It is also recommended that magnets should not be used during pregnancy. This is because there has not yet been sufficient research done in this field and also the baby's needs may be different from the carrying mother's needs.

If you are in any doubt about using magnets consult a specialist in this field who will advise you.

Recommended Reading

The relevant books recommended for this form of alternative therapy are:

Beaulieu, John. *Polarity Therapy Workbook*. Biosonic Enterprises, Ltd. New York New York 1994. ISBN 0-9640604-0-X

Brodie, Renee. *The Healing Tones of Crystal Bowls*. Aroma Art Ltd: 548-48 Street, Delta BC Canada V4M 2N3 1996. ISBN 0-9680790-0-8

Campbell, Don. *Music & Miracles*. Illinois: Quest Books, Wheaton Illinois 60189-0270, 1992. ISBN 0-8356-0683-X

Dewhurst-Maddock, Olivea. *The Book of Sound Therapy – Heal Yourself with Music and Voice*. New York: Simon & Schuster, Inc; 1993. ISBN 0-671-78639-3

Eden, Donna. *Energy Medicine*. Piatkus: 5 Windmill St., London W1P 1HF 1999 ISBN 0-7499-1928-0

Gimbel, Theo. *Form, Sound, Colour & Healing*. Essex: U.K., C.W. Daniel Co. Ltd.

Gimbel, Theo. *Healing with Colour & Light*. New York: Simon & Schuster, Inc., 1994. ISBN 0-671-86857-8

Goldman, Jonathan. *Healing Sounds*. Massachusetts: Element Books, Rockport, MA 01966. 1992. ISBN 1-85230-314-X

Lacy, Marie-Louise. *Know Yourself Through Colour*. London: The Aquarian Press, Harper Collins, 85 Fulham Palace Rd. London W6 8JB 1989.

Melody. *Love is in the Earth*. Earth-Love Publishing House, 3440 Youngfield St., Suite 353, Wheat Ridge, Colorado 80033 USA. 1995 ISBN 0-9628190-3-4

Stewart, R.J. *Music & the Elemental Psyche*. The Aquarian Press, Harper Collins, 85 Fulham Palace Rd., London W6 8JB ISBN 0850304946

Wall, Vicky. T*he Miracle of Colour Healing*. Aquarian/Thorsons Press, London. 1990. ISBN 1-85538-289 -X